LifeCaps Presents

Mister Rogers

A Biography of the Wonderful Life of Fred Rogers

By Jennifer Warner

BOOKCAPS

BookCaps™ Study Guides

www.bookcaps.com

Table of Contents

About LifeCaps

LifeCaps is an imprint of BookCaps™ Study Guides. With each book, a lesser known or sometimes forgotten life is recapped. We publish a wide array of topics (from baseball and music to literature and philosophy), so check our growing catalogue regularly (**www.bookcaps.com**) to see our newest books.

Introduction

Fred Rogers was one of the most beloved children's television hosts during the 1960's through the 1990's. He was most famous for his show, Mister Rogers' Neighborhood, where he talked to children directly through the television in his trademark slow manner of speech and zippered cardigans.

The compassionate persona he emitted through the television was not an act, as Fred Rogers the person deeply cared about children and their education. He viewed television as not mere entertainment, but as a tool for self-reflection as well as a means of real communication. His genuine way of communicating with not only children, but also adults, touched the hearts of everyone he met, and his legacy of kindness has since been passed on by those who knew him.

Chapter 1: Childhood and Education

Family and Early Years

Frederick Rogers was born on March 28, 1928 to James and Nancy Rogers at his grandparents' house in Latrobe, Pennsylvania. His mother was the only child of Fred McFeely, who later became Fred's closest relative.

His parents were intensely religious, and Fred grew up highly influenced by the Christian faith. His father worked at the family brick company and taught Fred Rogers his valuable work ethic. The company was called the McFeely Brick Company, and was started by Fred's grandfather. Eventually, James Rogers bought the company and took over the leadership responsibilities for the elder McFeely.

His mother, Nancy, frequently volunteered at the hospital as a nurse's aide and loved taking care of people. Both his mother and father were well known and well-loved in the town. Fred had many memories of his mother's caring nature, including watching her take care of World War II troops and making everyone in their family hand knit sweaters every Christmas. Because of his mother, Fred developed a fondness for sweaters and always requested a zippered one for the next year. These were the same sweaters that he eventually became known for wearing on Mister Rogers' Neighbourhood, and, according to his interview with Karen Herman, until his mother died every single sweater he wore on the show was hand knit by her.

He grew up in Pittsburgh with a particularly large family but was especially close to his grandparents during his childhood years. He spent long days with his grandfather, who allowed him to roam, play and express himself freely in a way that had an impact on Fred Rogers even when he became older. In his interview for Emmy TV Legends, he recalls one memory in which his grandfather told him that he made his day better just by being himself. This, of course, made Fred feel truly special and loved. When he became older, he still remembered that feeling and made it his mission in life to pass it on to others.

When Fred was eleven, his parents adopted a six month old baby girl whom they named Elaine, and Fred became an older brother. He tremendously enjoyed having a sibling, and Elaine turned out to be quite a mischief maker. It was rumoured that one of the puppets on his television show, Mister Rogers' Neighbourhood, was named after Elaine.

Hobbies and Interests

As a child, Fred had a lot of trouble expressing his feelings. He often felt isolated from other children, and sometimes even adults. He got sick often, and was made fun of for being overweight. His shy and quiet nature didn't help him connect with other children, and when he expressed his frustration to the adults in his family they advised him to ignore the negative feelings. This hurt Fred and only served to make him more confused. As a television host, he tried to get across to parents and children that ignoring feelings never solved any problems and that children needed to find a way to get those feelings out.

The outlet that Fred eventually found for his frustration and other negative feelings was the piano. As a remarkably young child, it was his mother who played the piano for him, but by the age of five he began to be able to play himself. He showed great promise as a musician and enjoyed playing the piano for others, as well as putting on puppet shows. Because it was hard for him as a child to put his often confusing and muddled feelings into words, the piano allowed him to express himself in a way that didn't hurt anyone else. As an adult, he tried to pass on that knowledge to other children. He emphasized that it didn't have to be the piano, but could be any form of artistic expression from music to art or acting.

It was his grandmother who gave him his first piano, a twenty five dollar pump organ that he played on all the time as a child. In his interview, he recalls that the only time when he felt like he was his true self was when he was playing music. He did, however, have other hobbies besides the piano and his passion for music. He was also obsessed with photography, a hobby that he entertained until the end of his life. As a child, he would often go down to the basement dark room and develop his pictures himself. When he got older, he had his photographs developed elsewhere. Unlike many photographers, Fred was not interested in capturing landscapes or objects, but rather people. He loved nothing more than to photograph the expressions on people's faces.

Religion

Fred was born into a deeply religious family, and his mother and father were hugely involved in the church when he was growing up. The family attended the First Presbyterian Church of Latrobe every week and even as a young child Fred was seriously engaged by the whole experience. He loved listening to the sermons, even when others were bored, and felt as though religion touched something in him. Religion helped shaped Fred's view that every individual has a unique and perfect purpose in life, no matter their situation, and helped him pursue a life of kindness and generosity.

This also may have had something to do with his father, who was a generous person and believed that the church should always give back to the community more than it received. Fred grew up learning this valuable lesson, and spent the rest of his life giving back, to children and adults alike, through the medium of television.

High School

Fred's shyness and lack of confidence, despite his loving family and church support, followed him into his high school years. He felt isolated from others his age, and this isolation caused him to shrink back in school. Several unlikely friendships, however, during these years, forever changed Fred's relationship with himself and others.

One of these friendships was with a popular, talented athlete named Jim Stumbaugh. During school, Fred never dreamed that he and Jim would ever be the type to become friends. One day, however, Jim was injured during a game and had to spend an extended time in the hospital. Fred was assigned the task of delivering Jim's homework to him, taking notes for him during class, and making sure he had all the books he needed to keep up while he was bedridden.

Throughout Jim's hospital stay, he and Fred got to know each other. Fred could see past Jim's popular sports guy exterior, and Jim appreciated Fred for his quiet and kind nature. The two became remarkably close friends, and continued their friendship even after Jim was released from the hospital and allowed to go back to school. It was the first time that it was possible for someone his age to take the time to learn about the depth of Fred's personality, and allow himself to be known by Fred in return.

When Jim returned back to school, he told others that Fred wasn't too bad, opening the door for the other students to get to know and appreciate Fred, as well. Fred gained confidence in himself, and learned first-hand the lesson that he tried to pass along to children in his television show - just to be yourself without shame. It was the same lesson his grandfather taught him as a child, but the first time that Fred truly understood what a difference it could make in someone's life.

The boost in confidence allowed Fred to take more risks in his school and home life, and soon he was hugely involved in school activities. By the end of his senior year of high school, Fred was the editor of the yearbook, in charge of the school newspaper, as well as president of the student council. He was well known and well-liked by his classmates and teachers, and while he still kept his quiet personality, he came to be respected for it instead of mocked.

Another unlikely friendship that changed Fred was his friendship with George Allen. George was a friend of the family and an African American. His two passions were flying and music, and he shared these passions with Fred. George was a member of a Piper Club in high school, and taught Fred how to fly. It was not something that Fred was especially interested in, but he was struck by the enthusiasm with which his friend talked about flying and wanted to pass that knowledge to someone else. It was then that Fred realized what it meant to be a true teacher, and George's passion for flying infected Fred, making him want to learn how to fly, as well. The two kept in touch throughout their lives, and George Allen later became a pilot and a jazz musician.

College

When Fred graduated high school and attended college, he had no major plans other than going to seminary and becoming a minister. He felt as though religion was his true calling, and would allow him to touch many people throughout his life. He still desired a college degree, however, and enrolled in Dartmouth College for his freshman year. Since he did not know exactly what to study, he decided to focus on another one of his passions - language. Specifically, the romance languages.

After his first year of higher education, however, he decided that he actually wanted to study music. A teacher of his told him that Dartmouth didn't have a program that was worth Fred's talent, and suggested for Fred to check out the music program at Rollins College. Fred took his advice, and on his next break signed up for a tour of Rollins. It was on this tour that he met his future wife, Sara Joanne Byrd. He impressed Joanne with his musical ability, and became fast friends with her and her group.

Fred transferred to Rollins the very next year, stating later that he felt at home at Rollins College more than he ever did at Dartmouth. He remained passionate about his music and majored in music composition as well as minoring in French language. It was also during his years at Rollins that he had his first acting experience. A teacher encouraged him to try stage drama. It was a role that he never actually wanted, as he preferred working quietly in the background to being the center of attention.

By 1951, Fred Rogers was a senior at Rollins College, and about to graduate. He still planned on becoming ordained, and had plans to go to the Pittsburgh Theological Seminary the following fall. However, everything changed when he went home on break and he experienced television. He had never experienced the medium before, and the first show he ever saw had two men throwing pies at each other's faces. Fred was both appalled and engrossed by the television show. He realized that the technology of television could be a fantastic medium for reaching out to people and educating them. However, he was greatly upset at seeing such a medium being abused. He was so upset, in fact, that he changed his mind about going to seminary and decided to try and get a career in television instead. This sudden change of plans put Fred on track to become the Mister Rogers that children all over the world knew and loved.

Fred's Connection to Childhood

One of the reasons that Fred Rogers became such a success in the children's television world is that, even as an adult, he had a remarkable connection to his own childhood. Where many adults forget what it is like to be a child, Fred made it a point to remember, and was able to see things from a child's perspective. Because of this, Fred was able to connect with children directly and meaningfully.

There were many instances in his childhood and young adulthood that stuck with Fred, even after growing up, and influenced the messages that he tried to pass on to children and adults in his television show. The things that affected Fred the most centered on feeling and being himself. As a child, Fred was full of conflicting emotions. He did not know how to express himself, and adults told him to ignore his feelings, and they would go away. Eventually, Fred realized that it was okay, and even perfectly normal, to have negative feelings and wanted to share that with the children on his show. He believed that, many times, problematic miscommunications between parents and children were caused by not understanding these feelings and having no outlet with which to express them.

Another facet from his childhood that stuck with Fred and influenced his life's work was the confidence he received when someone appreciated him for simply being himself. This happened first with his grandfather, Fred's closest relative as a child, who astounded Fred by appreciating him, not for doing anything special or extraordinary, but just for being Fred. This same theme came up in high school, when Fred was accepted by the popular athlete Jim, and once again Fred experienced a boost of confidence and happiness from this acceptance.

Fred never lost or forgot these valuable experiences, and they shaped every interaction he had both on the television and off it. For many, these experiences may have seemed insignificant; but for Fred Rogers, they shaped his very person and life mission.

Chapter 2: Early Television Work

Starting Out at NBC

After Fred Rogers graduated from Rollins College armed with his new degree in music composition, he contacted NBC in New York City asking if they had any positions open. They decided to hire the promising young man as an assistant to the producer Charles Polacheck, and Fred moved to New York that very year to begin working. He began his first official day at NBC on October 1, 1951.

As an assistant, Fred spent much of his first year running errands for the producer and other television workers. In the early years, the entire NBC television staff took up one floor of the building; a far cry from the massive production companies in modern day. In his Emmy TV Legends Interview, Fred recalls some defining learning experiences from his early years as an assistant. In one instance, he learned how a person's true nature is revealed when they are being served. He vividly remembered being harshly chastised for forgetting sweetener in someone's coffee, and realized then that the negativity in people affected their work, as well as the tone of the entire team.

The negative reactions affected him strongly, and he did all he could to bring a positive, engaging attitude to his work at NBC. At the time, he never had any inkling that his beginning in television would put him on the path to become famous. That was never something that he wanted, or even dreamed could happen. Nevertheless, working at NBC set the stage for his entire career and helped launch him into fame.

The most influential show for Fred at NBC was the Opera Theatre. The television station collaborated with famous composers to put on live operas that were then broadcast across the nation. Fred was enraptured at the musical experience, and had the privilege of working on the Opera Theatre when he became a floor manager. The Opera Theater was especially important to Fred because of his passion for both music and teaching. Although he did not work on the Opera Theater very long, he described it as the defining aspect of his work at NBC. He enjoyed listening to the operas performed over and over, until eventually he had them utterly memorized.

As a floor manager, Fred was in charge of timing the programs, making sure the cameras were ready, and letting the actors know when to start and stop. Since television was recorded live, this job was hugely important, and Fred excelled at it because of his attentive personality and his ability to thrive while working in the background of the shows.

In addition to working on the Opera Theatre, Fred Rogers was also the floor manager for many others shows, including The Kate Smith Hour, the Gabby Hayes Show, and The Hit Parade. Each of these shows were valuable learning experiences for Fred, and showed him the many ways in which television could be used. He immensely enjoyed working on The Kate Smith Hour because Miss Smith, a famous singer, had an amazing voice that Fred could listen to all day. During the Gabby Hayes show, Fred learned the importance of making television personal by watching Hayes, the host of the old western film show, talk to the camera as if there was only one person on the other side.

Eventually, however, Fred began to feel as though his position as floor manager at NBC didn't make full use of his many talents. The television culture was moving away from education and losing its original focus. He enjoyed his work, and was close to the staff at NBC, but became restless. Looking back, Fred valued his time at NBC because it not only taught him the mechanics of television work, but allowed him to develop deep relationships in the television community. In the end, however, he decided to leave in order to pursue his calling of music and educational television.

WQED and the Children's Corner

In 1952, the year after Fred began working at NBC, he and his young wife, Joanne, heard about a new station that was getting ready to broadcast in Pittsburgh. He found out about the news from his father, who lived real close to Pittsburgh in Fred's childhood home town, Latrobe. Even though the station was not even on the air yet, Fred felt an intense pull towards the educational program. This was helped by the fact that the station was being broadcast near his hometown, and Fred took this as a sign, or fate.

In 1953, Fred applied to the new station, named WQED, and was one of the first employees hired. He was offered a job as the program manager, and felt as though the job was his calling. Everyone at NBC could not believe that Fred was leaving just when his promising career at NBC was getting started. They didn't understand why Fred, who could eventually end up a producer at NBC, would quit to move to a small start-up station. Fred, however, was set on the move.

In November of 1953, Fred and Joanne moved to Pittsburgh in order to begin working for WQED. The station was at the forefront of community broadcasting, and, in fact, was the first community station in the entire country. This was hugely exciting for Fred, who felt as though he was finally getting a chance to work in meaningful education.

In the beginning, the show that Fred first became well known for, The Children's Corner, was not even one of the programs at the station. A month before the station was set to premiere, the manager realized that a children's show would be a beneficial addition to the programming line-up. Fred and a young woman named Josie Carey volunteered to come up with a children's show before April 1st, the date on which the station would air for the first time. At the time, Josie was working as the station secretary, but also had acting talent. The two became co producers and began creating The Children's Corner together.

Because the budget was so tight, and the time to create the set so short, The Children's Corner began as a remarkably simple endeavor. The show was scheduled to do an hour of programming a day, five days out of the week, which was a lot of content for such a small station. To fill their time quota, the co-producers decided to find free educational films aimed at children and present them on the show. The setup of the show was simple; Fred and Josie made the set out of a sheet which was painted with objects and places. During the show, Fred would work behind the scenes on the music, while Josie would be in front of the stage singing and presenting the short films. Originally, Josie was the only character on the show. It was only later that the puppets were added.

The station successfully aired its first program on the April 1st, 1954 - an hour long preview of the station shows. The first official content aired a few days later, on Monday, April 5th. On April 4th, the night before the station was set to air, the director of WQED, Dorothy Daniel, threw a party for all the employees to celebrate. At the party, Fred was given a present, a small tiger puppet he promptly dubbed "Daniel" in honor of the director.

Just like the creation of The Children's Corner itself, the addition of puppets as regular characters on the show was totally accidental. On the first day of the show, Fred wanted to use the puppet once in order to thank Dorothy and possibly make her laugh. So, he cut a slit in the sheet, right in the middle of a painted grandfather clock. The next day during the premiere show, Daniel came out of the clock and began talking to Josie, who was hosting. Fred only thought to use the puppet once, but Daniel was a huge success with the audience, who wanted to see him more. Fred was surprised but happy; he had played with puppets as a child but had not followed that hobby into adulthood. This gave him an opportunity to express himself creatively, and to engage in very real interactions with Josie on the show even though he worked back stage.

Daniel became a regular member of the cast, and Fred believes that the addition of puppets is what really saved the show. Every day, Daniel would come out of the clock in the middle of the set and talk with Josie about anything and everything. Nothing was scripted beforehand, so the conversations were completely live and real. Daniel eventually became so popular that Fred decided he wanted to add more puppet characters to the show.

The next character that The Children's Corner introduced was named King Friday, a sad king who lost his country, called Calendar Land, and whose birthday was on Friday the 13th. Every Friday the 13th The Children's Corner would celebrate King Friday's birthday, which the children always found fun. After King Friday, even more puppets were added, including X the Owl and Lady Elaine, whom many speculate was named after Fred's sister. In addition to involving the puppets in the show, Fred and Josie often asked special guests from the community to come and talk. They asked people who worked in interesting places, or knew a lot about specific subjects. There were certainly no requirements, just as long as the co-producers believed that the children would find it interesting and informative.

As The Children's Corner gained in popularity, Fred became more and more involved in the show. Not only was he in charge of playing the music behind the scenes, but as the puppetry became more involved Fred took on those responsibilities, as well. He found that, in order to get from the organ to all the different puppets, he had to almost run because of the live nature of the show. Fred began wearing his signature tennis shoes behind the scenes, so that his footsteps would be quieter and he would be more comfortable. He never gave his choice of shoes much thought, and, like his signature puppets and zip up sweaters, the tennis shoes just became a part of his persona naturally.

On top of his duties on the air, Fred was also in charge of writing the melodies for songs and collaborating with Josie to come up with words. Fred immensely enjoyed the musical nature of the show, and wanted the children who watched it to learn valuable life lessons as well as explore the world around them. As the show developed, the set became more and more fanciful. They added a tree and a castle, and Fred even appeared on air one time masked as Prince Charming. Fred had no desire to be on camera, and was happy working behind the scenes. He and the other members of the staff ran the show with an enthusiastic attitude and a focus on fun.

Eventually, the show became so successful that Fred and Josie became local celebrities, and NBC even took notice of the show. They invited Fred and Josie to perform for them in New York when their head of religious programming left on a four week vacation, leaving an open slot on Saturday mornings that needed to be filled. For one month, Fred and Josie travelled to New York City every Friday night, performed live on Saturday morning, and flew back in time to make the Monday morning program of The Children's Corner in Pittsburgh.

The show was a hit on NBC as well, and the station received over a hundred thousand letters about the show during the temporary time that it was being aired. Due to the success, NBC asked them to become regulars since the show was such a record breaking success. NBC had larger puppets made of all the characters, including Daniel and King Friday, and these were the puppets that were later used on Mister Rogers' Neighbourhood.

When the duo became regulars on NBC, they were given the opportunity to move back to New York and make The Children's Corner an enormous success. Both Fred and Josie, however, wanted to stay located in Pittsburgh. The travel was hard on both of them, but they felt as though they couldn't leave WQED. Fred and Josie worked on The Children's Corner together for a total of eight years before they both moved on to other projects.

Seminary on the Side

During his eight years of working on The Children's Corner, Fred made the most of his time by pursuing his original passion for religion during his lunch breaks. He attended the Pittsburgh Theological Seminary and put in as much study as his work would allow. Even though he had a promising career in television, he still was not able to give up his original dream of doing something influential in the religious sphere. He did not, however, plan on becoming a traditional minister, but wanted to continue his television work using his Masters of Divinity.

It was during his years at seminary school that Fred had his first experience truly studying childhood development. The most influential course he took was a masters counseling course with Dr. Margaret McFarland, who later became one of his closest professional friendships. During the course, he was assigned a child to work with for the whole semester, with McFarland supervising him. McFarland was in charge of the Arsenal Family and Children's Center, a center dedicated exclusively to studying child development.

During his classes in child development, Fred experimented with puppet interaction. He would bring in puppets and watch how the children talked and interacted with them. Watching the children, he realized that they behaved totally differently with puppets than with real people, and that it was easier to open up and communicate through the puppets. Although he had used puppets in The Children's Corner, he never thought about how the children would perceive them differently and how he could use them for educational purposes until his work with the children at the center.

In 1962, Fred was finally ordained by the church, with his vocation being to work with children and families through the mass media, specifically, television. He planned on putting on a new show for the Presbyterian Church, but plans for the program kept being delayed due to lack of funding. Although he was doing it for the Presbyterian Church, this new show was not supposed to be overly religious. Rather, Fred wanted to use his knowledge about children, families and communication to help his audience work through difficult issues in ways that were not harmful, as well as explore the world around them more fully. The Church saw the benefits in not mentioning religion specifically on the show, and believed that the Holy Spirit was behind Fred and would talk through him to his audience.

While Fred was struggling to get his new program started, he received a life changing call from Fred Rainsberry.

Misterogers Is Born

It was the day after his commencement that Fred received the call from Rainsberry, who was in charge of children's programming in Canada. He had seen Fred work with children, and thought he had a particularly special gift for communicating with them in a meaningful way. He wanted Fred to come to Canada and put on a fifteen minute children's program using puppets and Fred's musical talent. Taking a chance, Fred moved his family, including he and Joanne's two young boys, to Toronto to begin working on the new show. Fred realized it was a leap of faith, but couldn't help but feel it was fate that Rainsberry had called the very day after he was ordained to offer him a new job in his vocation.

When Fred arrived in Canada and began working on the development of the show, he was shocked to find out that Rainsberry wanted Fred to be on camera instead of behind the scenes with the puppets. Since Fred had no desire to be on screen, and preferred his work in the back ground, he was truly reluctant to put Rainsberry's plan into action. Rainsberry, however, had seen Fred work with children face to face, and wanted that same sort of interaction on the show. He truly believed that Fred had a talent for connecting with children, and knew that if he could get that across over the air then the show would be a hit.

After a year of brainstorming and preparation, Fred and Rainsberry were ready to start the new show, which Rainsberry named Misterogers. Rainsberry thought that naming the show after Fred Rogers would establish him as the centre of the program, and that keeping it one word would help it feel less formal. This would allow the children to be more open to what Fred had to say, and view him more as a friend and guide than an adult telling them what to do.

The show was set up with Mister Rogers in a neighborhood with whimsical sets and puppets to interact with. Fred brought along his favorite puppets from his early days working on The Children's Corner, and a man named Ernie became the puppeteer, with Fred talking on stage. During the show, Fred would invite guests to do interviews, much as he did on The Children's Corner. The only difference was it was Fred on stage talking instead of Josie.

The show was a sweeping success in Canada, and after the initial one year contract was up, Fred had to decide whether or not to stay in Canada with the new show or move his family back to Pittsburgh and search for another job. While he and his wife enjoyed Toronto, they both decided to move back to the states so that they could be closer to family. They also wanted to find a place to stay and raise their two boys, who were still young.

Chapter 3: Mister Rogers' Neighbourhood

Creation of Mister Rogers' Neighbourhood

After deciding to leave Canada and Misterogers in order to go back to the states, Fred began looking for a television job in Pittsburgh. At first he could not find a job in broadcasting, and so got an education job in the church working with children. However, he kept his passion for television and waited patiently for WQED to create another children's program.

During this in between stage, Fred also did small projects for his television connections. He worked on a few Christmas programs, and even did a commercial. Fred was glad to work in television but didn't enjoy doing the commercial because of his concern with selling products to children, who were always much more impressionable than adults. Even later, when he became the host of Mister Rogers' Neighbourhood, he made it a point never to pitch anything to the children in his audience, believing, perhaps rightly so, that doing so would violate their trust in him.

In 1965, only a year after leaving Canada, Fred prepared a short children's program for WTAE in Pittsburgh that aired on Sunday afternoons. Even though the show only ran for three months, from October to December, it allowed Fred to get back into the broadcasting world in Pittsburgh and gave him the opportunity to get to know and admire people who, later, he would work with on Mister Rogers' Neighbourhood.

After waiting patiently for two years, the funding finally became available for Fred to do his own children's show in Pittsburgh. Mister Rogers' Neighbourhood had finally begun, and Fred began preparing for the new show. They decided to use the footage from Misterogers in Canada, and got the rights to the old shows. However, Misterogers consisted of fifteen minutes of programming, and the slot that WQED needed to fill was half an hour. To make up for the time difference, they added short films in the middle of the episodes, using Fred on camera to transition from the original show to the short films. Mister Rogers' Neighbourhood officially premiered in Pittsburgh during the October of 1966.

While the first year of the show was successful, it was essentially a rehash of the Canadian Misterogers. The only "new" material to the show was the transitions into the short films and the films themselves. It was during this time, however, that Fred coined the Neighbourhood of Make-Believe and established the basic format of Mister Rogers' Neighbourhood.

Mister Rogers Goes National

After the first year of Mister Rogers' Neighbourhood had been broadcast in Pittsburgh, the Eastern Educational Network (EEN) wanted to expand the original programming for one hundred more shows. The network would also help broaden the area in which the show was broadcast, adding coverage in major cities such as Washington D.C., New York, San Francisco, Miami, and Boston.

It wasn't certain that the show would expand that far, however, as funding was still an issue. As a publicity stunt, and to try and attract funds, an open house was held in Boston featuring Mister Rogers' Neighbourhood. When over two hundred times the amount of people they planned for showed up, totalling over ten thousand throughout the day, it gained enough attention that the Sears Company agreed to fund the production of the show for the selected cities.

In October of 1967, Fred began taping new content for the first national season of Mister Rogers' Neighbourhood. He began expanding on the original show, writing the famous opening song "Won't You Be My Neighbour" which remained the opening for the duration of the show. He also added one of his favorite songs written by Josie called "Tomorrow" which was used as the first ending. During the production process, Fred consulted with his old professor, Margaret, on how to incorporate child development issues smoothly into the show in ways that the children in the audience would understand. Margaret was more than happy to help, and she continued acting as a consultant to Fred and the Neighbourhood until her death.

The revamped show also added more characters, puppets, and places to visit. Instead of just showing short videos, Fred would go out of the studio and explore a new place each episode. A new music director was hired named Jonny Costa, and later the music section also expanded to include a guitarist, bass player, and percussionist. There were also three regular puppeteers hired for the show to accommodate the growing amount of puppets. New props were made, new sets built, and finally Mister Rogers' Neighbourhood was ready for its first national broadcast.

First Run

The premiere episode of the new and improved show was broadcast on National Educational Television on February 19, 1968. The first season totaled out at one hundred and thirty episodes. This was when color television was first being made, so the early episodes were produced and aired in black and white. The next year, the show produced the second season of the Neighbourhood in color for the first time. Also, after the first season, the episode numbers were trimmed from one hundred and thirty to sixty five. This format continued for the duration of the first run of Mister Rogers' Neighbourhood.

The show continued production, and only gained in popularity. It wasn't until the third season, in 1970, when the National Educational Television station stopped broadcasting, and the series was taken over by Public Broadcasting Service (PBS). Even though the station underwent a major transformation, Mister Rogers' Neighbourhood never went off the air and eventually became closely associated with PBS.

The first run of Mister Rogers' Neighbourhood continued production for a total of eight complete seasons, and four hundred and fifty five episodes. At this point, Mister Rogers decided to take a break from the Neighbourhood, and production was halted in favor of doing reruns on PBS.

Reruns

In order to ease the transition between the first run and the reruns, the crew produced five episodes for the ninth season which aired in 1976. These were not typical episodes, as they were centred on Mister Rogers watching clips from older episodes in his workshop. The idea was to show children that watching the reruns would be fun, and make the change feel like a deliberate one. This way, Mister Rogers' Neighbourhood was able to halt production and transition smoothly into doing reruns.

Just because the episodes were reruns didn't mean that there was not any work to be done, however. Many of the earlier episodes were edited in parts or given new voices or video. This also gave Fred a chance to fix things that may have gone wrong during the first run of the show, or to correct things that turned out to be harmful or unproductive. The old episodes were aired on PBS during the same time slot as the old program and added a short note at the end of each episode mentioning the show's sponsors, as well as the number of the episode.

Second Run

After a few years, it was decided to bring Mister Rogers' Neighbourhood back into production. However, since so many episodes from the first run were still relevant, there was no need to create one hundred or sixty five episode seasons. Instead, Fred decided to focus on producing a more manageable fifteen episodes per season, and tied them together more strongly.

During the first run, each episode was a standalone episode, focusing on a specific topic for a short period of time. For the second run, the show focused on linking together episodes by week and focusing on one principal theme the entire time. Fred believed that by not having the episodes stand alone, it would create more depth and extend the story beyond the screen. It would also give children more time to process and think about the issues, and by leaving an episode open ended, let the audience use their imagination to fill in the rest using their own experience and feeling.

In this way, the show became more interactive with the children in the audience, and Mister Rogers challenged the children to think through things on their own. It was also important to Fred because he emphasized that children had their own individuality and that each child had a story to tell. Filling in the blanks was one way for them to tell their own story instead of listening to someone else's.

Some of the topics covered during these episodes included serious issues such as divorce and loneliness, as well as fun ones such as opposites. Each topic was developed in depth through Mister Rogers' talks, the field trips, and especially in the Neighbourhood of Make Believe.

From 1979 to 1993, fifteen new episodes were produced per season. From there, the number of episodes per season became abundantly irregular, ranging from five to twenty episodes. The program continued running from 1994 until the show's final season, consisting of only five episodes, in 2001. During this time, many of the older episodes, including the entire first season, stopped being aired because they were so old. The new material produced during the second run served to counteract the loss of the earlier shows, making it so that the program could run indefinitely.

Special Programs

Because of his national success, in 1971 Fred was able to form a corporation called Family Communications in order to create more projects. This gave him as well as other members of the Neighbourhood crew a chance to expand beyond the neighboorhood and do special projects. Many of these projects dealt with issues that were difficult or frightening for children. Fred covered everything from serious illness to going to the dentist, and wanted to present himself as a friend and guide for children in those sensitive situations.

In addition to the short videos produced by Family Communications, Fred also organized a yearly opera, which took place only in the Neighbourhood of Make Believe and lasted for an entire thirty minute episode. The first opera special aired in 1968, and the tradition continued until there were a total of thirteen opera specials. At the beginning of the opera episode, Fred would do a brief introduction before taking the audience to the Neighbourhood of Make Believe. The main actor in these operas was a famous American singer named John Reardon. Because of his limitless passion for music, the opera specials were some of Fred's favorite work on Mister Rogers' Neighbourhood. It is possible that the opera specials came to be because of Fred's experiences while working on NBC's opera theatre, which reaffirmed his belief, that music should be an integral part of television.

Perhaps one of Mister Rogers more famous specials was the Christmas special, titled Christmastime with Mister Rogers. The special had the same basic format as the other episodes of Mister Rogers' Neighbourhood, but also featured a guest storyteller. After the storyteller, they travelled to the Neighbourhood of Make Believe, where the puppets were also celebrating Christmas. This special was aired every year at Christmas from 1977 to 1982.

Format of the Show

The format of Mister Rogers' Neighbourhood, although expanded considerably since its initial conception as Misterogers, remained exceedingly simple throughout its entire run. Part of this was due to the simple, ritualistic personality of Fred Rogers himself.

When the show opened, it showed Mister Rogers singing "Won't You Be My Neighbour" to the audience while supposedly coming home from a day's work. At first he is in more formal clothing, but as he sings he makes himself comfortable in his "home", taking off his blazer and dress shoes, and putting on instead his famous zippered cardigans and laid back tennis shoes. By appearing in such a casual manner, Mister Rogers invited the audience to become comfortable as well, and immediately set a tone of trust and intimacy for the program.

After the introductory song, Mister Rogers always took some time to talk to the children directly. He never acted on his show, but always made an effort to be genuine and honest in front of the camera. He believed that children could tell when adults were being phony, and strove to only be himself while on the show. This was a valuable lesson Fred learned as a child, and he believed that nothing was more important than teaching other children that lesson. His way of teaching this was through example, as his audience grew up with him on his show.

Even though Mister Rogers spent a good deal of time talking directly to his audience, he made it a point to film something outside of the studio for most of the episodes. These "field trips" were all filmed beforehand, and then, back in the studio, Fred would do the transitions into them. The field trips could be anything, as long as Fred was able to show the children something interesting. This could be going to a crayon factory, visiting a bakery, or going to places such as hospitals or zoos. Anything that Fred thought might interest children he was willing to explore, and since children have an insatiable curiosity for the world and how things work, there was never a lack of possible material.

After the activity of the day, whether it be a field trip or guest interview, the attention of the show turned to the Neighbourhood of Make Believe. The transition from the real world on set to the Neighbourhood of Make Believe was always shown using a trolley that travelled into the Nneighbourhood. The trolley was very important to the show, because it was the only element that was constantly shown in both the real life set and the Neighbourhood. Rogers believed that it was hugely influential to make it obvious that the Neighbourhood of Make Believe was not set in reality, but rather a whimsical place where the characters could learn, explore, and act out different scenarios. This idea of separation between reality and fantasy was extremely unusual for children's shows, which often purposefully put the fantastic in a realistic setting.

In the Neighbourhood, an entire cast of puppets acted out scenarios. There were many puppeteers involved in the acting for the puppets throughout the series, and by the end of the series over fifty puppets had made appearances throughout the show. The scenes in the Neighbourhood of Make Believe always related to what had happened on the show during that episode, and allowed Fred to construct relevant, entertaining sstories in order to explore difficult issues. He had found during his study of child development that children interacted differently with puppets than with adults. Because the puppets were not human, but had their own voices and personalities, they were much more approachable and better at talking through sensitive subjects.

After the segment in the Neighbourhood of Make Believe was over, the camera followed the trolley back onto the set, where Mister Rogers was waiting to discuss what had happened in the Neighbourhood that day. Often throughout the course of the show, other characters in the "real" neighboorhood, as opposed to the Neighbourhood of Make Believe, would make appearances. These characters were based off of people that Fred knew in real life, and Mister Rogers would have interesting conversations with them on the air.

The entire show, from beginning to end, put a great emphasis on communication, exploring feelings, and opening up to others. By having both a "real life" neighboorhood cast, and a make believe neighboorhood, Mister Rogers' Neighbourhood was able to explore the topics of the day from many different angles and perspectives. As the show went on longer and longer, more and more characters were added, both in the "real" neighboorhood and the Neighbourhood of Make Believe. In total, there were almost fifty characters that made appearances on the show, not including the many guests that Fred invited to talk on the air.

While the show was geared towards preschool age children, between two and five, Mister Rogers did not neglect the parents. He knew that communication was a two way street and that both the parents and the child needed to learn to manage their feelings and communicate with each other in a positive manner.

After all the field trips, guests, and discussions had taken place, Mister Rogers ended the episode the way he began it, by singing another song. The episodes ended with the song "Tomorrow", written by Fred's co-producer on The Children's Corner, Josie, until 1973, when the show ran into copyright issues with a record company and were no longer able to use the original songs. Fred was forced to write a new song, which he titled "It's Such a Good Feeling". This song, in one form or another, was the ending of Mister Rogers' Neighbourhood until its very last season.

Themes of Mister Rogers' Neighbourhood

Part of the reason that Mister Rogers' Neighbourhood was able to continue running as long as it did was because Mister Rogers was not afraid to discuss any subject imaginable that would be relevant to children on the show. Because of his openness and honesty, he talked with his audience genuinely about issues both positive and negative, including the ones so sensitive that other children's shows avoided them with a metaphorical six foot stick.

Mister Rogers was famous for talking openly about significant life events that might impact a child, such as death or divorce. In 1970, during the third season of the show, Mister Rogers' pet goldfish died. On the show, Mister Rogers took the opportunity to explore not only the concept of death, but also how to handle the feelings of separation that go along with it. During the second run of the show, he featured an entire week on divorce and brought the issues over the Neighbourhood of Make Believe when Prince Tuesday was worried because his parents were not getting along.

In addition to major life events, Mister Rogers also discussed common childhood fears, from the highly irrational (going down the bathtub drain), to complicated child development issues such as permissible regression. Other fears, such as separation anxiety when parents left the house, and many more, were talked about in depth.

Not everything on the show was so serious, however, and Mister Rogers also focused on the passionate and fun aspects of life. He encouraged children to develop their imaginations to their fullest potential, and was famous for getting children to go outside, read, or do anything other than watch television. While Fred believed that the television was a terrific educational tool, he also realized that many children, as well as parents, used the technology as a crutch to replace actual interaction. That was part of the reason he made sure to include a segment or interview from outside the studio, to connect the show to the larger world outside. He wanted to keep children's curiosity alive and encourage them to explore and learn about the world around them on their own.

Ultimately, Mister Rogers' Neighbourhood was about teaching children about how to handle their feelings, and how to communicate those feelings in a positive way. For Fred, the way he found as a child was through music, which was why music was an integral part of Mister Rogers' Neighbourhood. Everything he did on the show was done to help the children, and parents in the audience better understand not only their own feelings and how to express them, but also how to understand the feelings of others. That was the most important lesson that Fred learned during his life, and the message that he wanted to spread to others so that they might be better equipped for their own journey.

Chapter 4: The End of an Era

Fred Rogers retired in 2001 at seventy three years old, after producing thirty one seasons and eight hundred and sixty five episodes of Mister Rogers' Neighbourhood. The retirement of Mister Rogers officially ended the production of the show, as there was no one who could possibly replace the beloved children's host.

Even though the show was no longer in production, PBS still continued to show reruns of the program on their network. It was not until 2008 that Mister Rogers' Neighbourhood was taken off of PBS's regular schedule. However, the show was still shown on the weekend, and other independent television stations continued to air the show because of its fame and popularity.

The Neighbourhood of Make Believe

Although the Neighbourhood of Make Believe only appeared for a short segment in each episode, it was an entire world with complex geography and characters. Each of the over fifty characters, both puppets and full-size costumed actors, had their own personalities, tendencies and backstories.

The Neighbourhood Regions

Although the set of the Neighbourhood was originally just a canvas sheet with painted locations on The Children's Corner, it continued to grow and evolve along with the show. By the time Mister Rogers was established, the Neighbourhood had many locations, regions, and even another planet. In the center of the geography was the Neighbourhood itself, but there were also four main regions, one for each cardinal direction.

To the west of the Neighbourhood was the City of Westwood, where Miss Sara Saturday lived before marrying King Friday XIII. Although Westwood was not shown very frequently, there were minor characters who continued to live there such as Mayor Maggie, Charles R. Aber and Mr. Skunk. Right after the colour episodes began airing, the Frogg family, which included Dr. and Mrs. Frogg along with their child Tadpole, moved to Westwood and were rarely seen on the show after that.

To the south was the City of Southwood, the home of Betty and James Jones and their adopted daughter Carrie Dell. Betty was a southern lady who was friends with Lady Elaine and often visited her in the Neighbourhood. Her husband, James, was actually her second husband and talked with an English accent.

North of the Neighbourhood, Northwood, consisted of mostly country and was inhabited by goats. The two main goats, Old Goat and New Goat, sometimes made appearances on the show. Old Goat could only speak using goat sounds, and so New Goat translated for him.

Lastly, to the west of the Neighbourhood was Someplace Else. This was the vaguest region, and also where the younger generation of puppets attended school. Their teacher, who lived in Someplace Else, was called Harriet Elizabeth Cow. There was also another character named Donkey Hodie who lived in the area, and whose name was a pun on the famous Spanish novel Don Quixote.

Completely separate from the Neighbourhood and its surrounding regions was Planet Purple, an alien planet where everything was purple, everyone had the same names, and everyone looked alike. The main character from Planet Purple was Purple Panda. He often visited the neighbourhood and interacted with the other characters in his monotone voice. Sometimes he was accompanied by Little Panda, who looked just like him, only smaller.

King Friday's Realm

Although the surrounding regions had many interesting characters and allowed for some variation during the Neighbourhood segments, most of the main characters and stories were told in the Neighbourhood itself. The Neighbourhood of Make Believe was ruled by King Friday XIII, who lived in the castle on the left of the set. Since the castle was on the left of the set, it was the first major landmark to be seen as the Trolley travelled into the Neighbourhood of Make Believe. There were two main areas of the Neighbourhood set, the area around the castle, and the area around the Oak Tree.

Surrounding the castle of King Friday XIII was the Eiffel Tower, home of Grandpedre Tiger. This location was modeled after the tower in Paris. The Tele Can was a phone booth, in which the "phone" was made of a can and string. Miss Paulifficate, a former dancer, was the operator, and often had interactions with the castle inhabitants. There was also a service entrance, a staircase, and a fountain. Near the service entrance of the castle was the Rocking Chair Factory, where Cornflake S. Pecially, a beaver character who first appeared on Mister Rogers, and his assistant, Hilda Pingleborder worked.

The castle itself was inhabited by King Friday XIII, the second puppet character ever created by Fred Rogers. King Friday XIII lost his kingdom, called Calendar Land, and made his new home in the Neighbourhood of Make Believe. He was the monarch and ruler of the Neighbourhood of Make Believe, and always spoke highly formally and habitually gave long speeches to whoever would listen. His birthday was celebrated every Friday the thirteenth on the show. In the second season, King Friday XIII married Queen Sara Saturday from Westwood, who was named after Fred's wife Sara Joanne. Queen Sara Saturday was much more organized that King Friday XIII, and was in charge of Food for the World. Their son, Prince Tuesday, was born during the third season and was one of the few characters who aged along with the show. Once he became older, he attended the school of Someplace Else along with the other young characters.

Other characters in the castle included Grandfather Thursday, King Friday's father, Edgar Cooke, the singing chef, and Lady Aberline, King Friday's niece and a full-size costume character. Aberline was next in line for the throne, and was one of the main characters in many of the Neighbourhood storylines.

The other main area of the Neighbourhood centred on the big Oak Tree, home to X the Owl, as well as Henrietta Pussycat, who lived in a school house lodged in the branches of the tree. X was the third puppet created by Fred Rogers, and was always eager to learn. Henrietta was a cat, and the fourth children's puppet on The Children's Corner.

Surrounding the Oak Tree was the Museum Go-Round, the Pond, and the Grandfather Clock. The Museum Go-Round was home to Lady Elaine Fairchild, who was, because of her somewhat irritable nature, often the bad guy of the various story lines. She was also named after Fred's sister, Elaine. The Museum Go-Round was always revolving and had a seemingly endless number of rooms. The Pond was originally home to the Frogg Family but was later replaced by the Platypus family, a large family of duck billed Platypus. Lastly, Daniel the Tiger inhabited the Grandfather Clock, which marked the end of the Neighbourhood of Make Believe. Daniel was the original puppet of the show, and a gift from Fred's director on The Children's Corner. He lived in the clock, had a shy personality, and always talked with Josie about her day during his first appearances.

Part of the Larger Picture

The Neighbourhood sections for the show were planned in advance and filmed all at once, and then tied in with the transitions from Mister Rogers on screen. Before the Neighbourhood of Make Believe segment of the show, Mister Rogers would always do an introduction, telling the audience what the skit was going to be about and relating it to what had already been talked about that day. After the show, he would then summarize the story and go into the issues in more detail if it was necessary.

Things that may have been too sensitive to talk about extensively live were more easily brought up in the make believe world. An example of this was the Kennedy Assassination, when the country was in turmoil. Fred relates during his Emmy TV interview how, through the Neighbourhood of Make Believe, both parents and children could learn to deal with the grief and confusion of the assassination. This was only one example of the power of the Neighbourhood of Make Believe in relation to Mister Rogers' audience.

This miniature world was Mister Rogers' whimsical dream-land, where anything could happen. He was always clear to strictly divide the Neighbourhood of Make Believe from the real world, but used the Neighbourhood characters to explore real world issues in a fun and non-imposing way for children. The way Fred described it was that he could talk about anything on camera but that anything could happen in the Neighbourhood of Make Believe.

Other TV Work

While he was the most famous for Mister Rogers' Neighbourhood, Fred Rogers also invested his time and energy into other work, as well. He was involved in the children's book business, held question and answer sessions for parents, and produced many specials featuring documentary or interview style interactions with upstanding members of the community.

The most notable of these specials are Fred Rogers' Heroes and Old Friends, New Friends. The latter was released in 1978, during the break between series one and two of Mister Rogers' Neighbourhood. Even though Fred Rogers was on sabbatical during his time away from the program, he didn't waste it, but rather focused on the creation of Old Friends, New Friends. For the show, Rogers travelled all over the United States talking to, interviewing, and videotaping interesting or admirable people. Fred Rogers' Heroes, aired in 1994, had a similar premise, but took four people and focused on them more intensely. The people documented included a school principal, a dancer, and even a farmer. Uncharacteristically on the show, Mister Rogers left his trademark zippered cardigan and tennis shoes at home, instead favoring a more formal suit and tie. Both of these shows were aired on PBS as sixty minute long specials.

While Fred Rogers did not host the parent specials sometimes aired before Mister Rogers Neighbourhood, he was the producer. He would answer questions from the audience, which consisted of parents and no children, in order to prepare parents for any potential questions or concerns their children may have had after watching the show that week. Unlike his other television appearances, these were directly connected to the content of Mister Rogers' Neighbourhood.

In addition to his numerous television projects, Fred Rogers also authored a total of thirty six children's books. While not directly connected to the show, the books dealt with common issues that children had, such as fear of going to the hospital or dealing with potty training.

Chapter 5: Family and Personal Life

Keeping true to the beliefs he instilled on his television show, Mister Rogers liked to keep his home life deep and simple. He began every morning by swimming, followed by a quiet period of reading and prayer. Fame never affected his life negatively, as he made sure to keep his healthy habits, including his vegetarian lifestyle and spending time with his family every night.

He met his wife, Sara Joanne Byrd, during his first year at Rollins College. Sara was an only child, and, like Fred, a talented musician. They were born the same year and shared an instant connection. Eventually, the two married and moved in together in New York. Although Joanne apparently wasn't good at cooking, the two still ate dinner together every night and often warmed up frozen food.

Other than his parents and grandparents, Fred was closest to his sister, Elaine, or affectionately called Laney. Elaine was eleven years younger than Fred, but the two still shared a bond. She grew up to be a water color artist, married, and had two sons. One of Fred's nephews taught music composition at Rollins College, and the other went to school to receive his doctorate. Fred enjoyed spending time with his nephews, and eventually, his grandchildren. He had a habit of taking the children of the family to the studio, where they would play and explore on the set.

Because of Fred's nature and job, his personal life and life on screen overlapped quite a bit. If something was bothering him that day, or if he was having problems at home, he could talk about them on the air with his audience. There were times, however, when his personal and private life collided. In his Emmy TV interview, Fred described the hardest moment of his performance career. It happened just after his father's death, when Fred had to do a series of twenty-three live performances directly after the funeral service. Even though Fred cried while singing "Won't You Be My Neighbour", he still finished all of the performances.

In the end, Fred's passion and purpose in life he felt was to help other people. Although he was extremely close to his family, he also considered his audience a very important part of his life. He involved himself with everyone he met, and always took the time to really listen to them. Because of this tendency, he rarely talked about himself extensively, letting his quiet, compassionate nature speak for him.

Advocacy Work

Because of Fred's passion for children and children's education, he was also very involved in advocacy work and became rather famous for his contributions to the world of children's programming. He began getting involved in advocacy work when he founded the non-profit organization called Family Communications, Inc. in 1971, soon after Mister Rogers' Neighbourhood had become a success. He did this for several reasons - one, to expand and give the cast and crew a space to pursue new projects, and two, so that he could better allocate the funds for the show.

In addition to founding non-profits for children's media, Mister Rogers also made his voice heard on a national level when he became involved in several government issues.

The first time Mister Rogers spoke in a government setting was 1969, just one year after the launch of his show on a national scale. The Nixon administration had proposed cutting the funding of the Public Broadcasting Services station by no less than ten million dollars, and Fred Rogers appealed to a group of senators in order to keep the funding. He famously appealed to the chairman of the group, a senator named John Pastore, who was famous for his tough guy attitude and impatient nature in his court proceedings.

During his appeal, Fred did not make traditional arguments but rather intensely engaged Pastore in a conversation about the importance of children's programming. He passionately conveyed his beliefs to the chairman that his show, and others on the network, helped children navigate their way through life and ultimately become, through education, better citizens and people. During the session, he even quoted songs from his own show in order to give an example of the content to Pastore, who had never watched Mister Rogers' Neighbourhood. At the end of the six minute speech, his passion had swayed the typically unpleasant senator, who gladly gave Mister Rogers' the funding plus another ten million. Although this was only one success in the world of children's education, it helped set a precedent in the broadcasting world and undoubtedly changed the way that government viewed public broadcasting in the future.

Another well-known instance where Mister Rogers appeared to the government on behalf of the education world was in the Supreme Court case between Sony and the Universal City Studio in 1984. Sony had made and marketed their new recording product called Betamax, which allowed the user to record television shows to watch at a later time. Although this technology has since become commonplace, at the time it was revolutionary and threatened to change the television world forever. Universal Studios, backed by the Hollywood industry, sued Sony for infringement of copyright, saying that by allowing home viewers to copy their programs Sony was responsible for the loss of material.

The case was a tough one for the Supreme Court, and many were called to testify and give their opinions on the complicated matter. Fred Rogers was one of these people. He told the Supreme Court his honest and unselfish opinion, that it would be better for viewers to be able to watch a program whenever it was convenient for them. In his case, he used the example of a family with children who, for one reason or another, could not watch his show because of time constraints. If instead the family could watch the show at their convenience, then the children would benefit from the education they received that they would not have otherwise. His opinion had an impact on the proceedings, because, as someone in the industry, the technology could possibly harm the network, and even his show. But, from Fred's point of view, he thought about the children and the audience rather than the financial aspect of the case.

These are merely a few examples of the many acts that Fred Rogers committed over the course of his lifetime in his effort to help improve the lives of children and families all over the nation. In each instance, his genuine and compassionate nature helped win over members of the government and industry alike, changing the impact of children's broadcasting for the positive in years to come.

Chapter 6: Death and Legacy

Fred Rogers retired from the television world after his last season of Mister Rogers' Neighbourhood aired in 2001. It was not long after that, in December of 2002, that he was diagnosed with stomach cancer. He still remained active, however, despite his diagnosis, even tossing the coin at the Rose Bowl on New Year's Day. This was to be his last public appearance, as he underwent a surgery later that month in an attempt to get rid of the stomach cancer. It was unsuccessful, however, and Mister Rogers spent the last month of his life at home, surrounded by his family and his loving wife. He died on February 27th, 2003, at seventy four years old.

His passing was mourned by the world, but most acutely by the communities of Pittsburgh and Latrobe. In honor of his life, the Pittsburgh newspaper published a full front page article celebrating him. His memorial was held in Pittsburgh as well, with over three thousand people attending, including famous television icons who admired his work. His body was buried in the Unity Cemetery of Latrobe.

After his death, PBS took steps to help children understand and cope with the loss of Mister Rogers, and did not stop airing his television show. Michael Keaton, an American actor, did a PBS special named Fred Rogers: America's Favourite Neighbour.

Even though he was no longer alive, Mister Rogers continued to touch those who knew him and worked with him, as well as the children and adults who watched his show. The studio that Mister Rogers' Neighbourhood was filmed at was renamed The Fred Rogers' Studio, and over the years buildings and statues have been dedicated to the man. At Saint Vincent College in Latrobe, the children's centre was named the Fred M. Rogers' Centre, and in Pittsburgh Robert Berks built a statue of Rogers. The children's museum in Pittsburgh also created a permanent exhibition about the life and works of Fred Rogers, and there was even a full size trolley ride made at a Pittsburgh amusement park that was an exact replica of the trolley on the Neighbourhood of Make Believe.

In addition to all the memorials, Fred Rogers received many awards both during his life and after his death. The most notable of these awards was the Presidential Medal of Freedom, awarded in 2002 by George W. Bush, his induction into the Television Hall of Fame in 1999, and his sweater being featured in the Smithsonian as a "treasure of American history". These are, in addition to his two George Foster Peabody awards, five Emmys, and many smaller awards received during his lifetime.

Numerous documentaries and books have also arisen from journalists, neighbours, and people who knew and admired Fred Rogers. Amy Hollingsworth, a journalist who met Fred Rogers during an interview and later became friends with him, wrote a book titled The Simple Faith of Mister Rogers. One of his real life neighbours filmed a documentary, Mister Rogers and Me, showing interviews with people who remembered the man or were influenced by him. Studies have been done about the way Fred interacted with people, especially journalists, and an article published in the Journal of Communication by Bishop analyses how everyone who met Fred ended up being friends with him. Bishop examined over a hundred articles and journals written by over eighty journalists, and found that the journalists were so affected by Mister Rogers that they, often purposely, lost all objectivity when they published their writing. This was a testament to the power of his personality, that anyone who met him, knew him.

Fred Rogers was an essential storyteller, and his stories were beyond any religion or any time period. His lessons are just as relevant today as they were when Mister Rogers' Neighbourhood was first aired in 1968, and his genuine love for children, and indeed, all humanity, caused everyone who met him to admire his presence. Even though the original Mister Rogers passed away, his legacy continues in the form of the people who were touched by his compassion and his simple, deep nature.

Bibliography

Books

The Simple Faith of Mister Rogers by Amy
Hollingsworth

I'm Proud of You: My Friendship with Fred
Rogers by Tim Madigan

The Wonder of It All: Fred Rogers and the Story
of an Icon by Margaret Mary Kimnmel,
Ph.D, and Mark Collins

Documentaries and Interviews

Mister Rogers and Me by Benjamin and
Christofer Wagner

Emmy TV Legends: Interview with Fred Rogers
Parts 1 - 9

Websites

Fredrogerscenter.org

imdb.org - Mister Rogers' Neighborhood

http://web.archive.org/web/20050103143529/www.wqed.org/mag/0403_remember3.shtml

http://www.pbs.org/parents/rogers/series/summary.html

http://www.biography.com/people/fred-rogers-9462161

Made in the USA
Lexington, KY
03 March 2018